Look, Really See: Introspective Poems About the Struggle to Grow Up as an Adult

Ashley Cohen

BookLeaf Publishing

Look, Really See: Introspective Poems About the Struggle to Grow Up as an Adult

Presentation by *BookLeaf Publishing*

Web: www.bookleafpub.com

E-mail: info@bookleafpub.com

ISBN: 9789357440783

First edition 2023

DEDICATION

For anyone that is struggling to simply get out of bed everyday, I see you

Untitled Document

The blinking line haunts me
Those 26 characters taunt me
I know I can always go back
I can undo any mistake
Spelling, grammatical, factual
I can backspace anything

So I should feel invincible
If there are no stakes
If there is a clear safety net
If there is no pressure to get it right the first time
I should just write all the time
I can always edit and revise
I should feel free to do anything
I can always start a new page
I should have already written this years ago
I can never go back in time

Part of me feels time already has slipped away
And I have nothing to show for it
Just the silent metronome of a vertical line
Pulsating to a tune that is not mine
The emptiness of the page
The blankness of endless possibilities
The vastness of no clear direction
I should revel in the freedom to write anything
But the freedom is overwhelming and I write nothing

I could be so great
With adoring fans
Be rich and famous
Like the ones on those magazine covers
People that are just everywhere
Where everyone knows their name
But I cannot be them
Because I am only this blank page
With all of the glory of an untitled document
In some obscure folder
Even if I want to be found
The finder would show no results

I want to skip the undos and redos
I want to just have the finished perfect work
Something so perfect that I will never have to worry
About any imperfections because it is exactly how I envision it
I want to skip all of the long hours
The pain in my fingers
The sacrifices having to be made
The energy it will take to even sit at a desk
The time wasted on things that will never happen

I should just get out of my own head
I can always just do it later
I should not worry if it turns out bad
I can always just do it tomorrow
I should have more self discipline
I can always try again later

Nobody Cares After the Fire

I heard there was a fire
Not too far from where I am now
I didn't know anyone in it
I didn't know anyone who knew anyone in it
But it was all anyone talked about
There were hashtags
Fame
Awareness
Celebrity
T-shirts

The fires were exceptionally bright
The orange and yellow flames
Reaching for the night sky
Tearing and clawing at it
The vertical lights became a beacon
Calling for innocent bystanders to come closer

Step right up and see
Come one, come all
Look how this building is permanently damaged
See the survivors barely holding on
See the flashes of camera lights
See how they neatly blend together with the flames

No one wants the fire to stop
Look at all the outrage and controversy
Look at the anger and blame and hatred

Look at all the energy that keeps the fire alive
What's the alternative?
Spend that energy finding solutions?
No
Too much actual effort
Waste time
Don't even think
Just keep the fire going

Look how it's bringing people together
The warmth is comforting
Don't think about the burns it's causing
At least being is warm is better than being cold
Fan the flames
Add more firewood
Because once the fire is out
No one will care about you anymore
A little spark caused all this destruction and pain
Be wary where you light the match

Playing Make Believe

Growing up I was told a lie
That I just have to try
To be as pretty as a supermodel
And I don't need to do anything with parents that coddled
And of course I need to be good at school
And always be on the lookout and not be a fool
If you see Prince Charming, horse and all
You'll be with him as soon as he accepts your call

Only nice things he will say
And will be there to always save the day
I will never have to work
Well maybe some light housework
He will love me, I will think
Because I am dressed up all in pink

We will live in his castle in the sky
And I will never ever again cry
All of my problems will magically disappear
Everything will be ok with my big strong man near
I am not capable of taking care of myself
So he will be in charge of my good health

No need for personality
No need for any kind of ability
As long as he loves me
Just for him and I to be
And together, I will finally be happy

F for Failure

I was good in school
I was good at getting good grades
All of my knowledge is gone now
But I will always have my big A+

I only participated for the grade
Not because I had something to say
I was the good girl with the good grades
The quiet girl, the nice girl
Who always knew what the homework was
Always knew precisely what to do
Where did she go?

Somehow waking up early everyday
To catch the bus so I wouldn't be late
Everyday for almost half of my life
Did not turn into a lifelong habit
I must have been a different person
Because now I rarely wake before noon

I thought grades were important
They were a reflection of me as a person
They were the source of my parents' pride
They let me know that I would become great
And now I'm grown up and I see
That I am recovering from burnout
From being an overachiever for so long

I think of the common question
"What do you want to be when you grow up?"
Conditioned as a child to want to contribute to
capitalistic coldness
Money becomes a sign that you are doing well
The smarter you are the more money you should have
School was supposed to guarantee my success
All of that time for a small piece of paper
All meaningless since I have not found my purpose

Some people pursue their passions
Some people travel the world
Some people change the world
Some people do everything they can to keep the
world the same
But that would require one to get out of bed

There are no more grades when school ends
No one to tell me what I should be doing
I only have myself to blame for
Why all of the 'shoulds' became 'did nots'
There are no more progress reports
No one to tell me that I am on the right track
Accountability ends at graduation

I barely have enough motivation to finish this poem
You read the final product
You do not see all of the distractions
The breaks, the naps, the snacks
My eyes drooping over my computer screen
This could have been better if I tried more
If I put more time and effort into this

Instead I’ll just end it here
With all of my potential for greatness
I settle for sleepy mediocrity

Contradictions of Young Adulthood

I do not know what I am
An adult that still acts like a teenager
A child playing make believe as a serious adult
Someone that still feels the need for approval
Someone that till recently had a whole life to look forward to
Someone that will never solve the puzzle of selfhood
A unique category of person in between it all

Is it possible to think that my life has ended before it ever began?
If only I picked a major in college
Or was in better extracurricular activities
Or took more leadership courses
Or gained the important skill of having something to be passionate about
Maybe then I would have a reason to wake up in the morning
Instead of barely being cognizant in the afternoon

I do not feel prepared to be an adult
There is so much that I never practiced before
Suddenly you graduate and suddenly you are supposedly capable
But my grandma still feels the need to call to inform me
Of the importance of wearing a coat when it is cold outside
If I can't decide to wear a jacket on my own
Why do they think I can do anything?

I want them all to leave me alone
They still see me and their little girl that needs protecting
I can never grow if they keep me in their clutches

They will all be gone eventually and I'll survive without their help
I cannot make my own choices because they were chosen for me
I never learned how to take initiative because they did all the work
I do not have a drive to be better because they are the safety net
That is always there to catch me whether or not I deserve to be caught

I put on a blazer and feel like a child playing dress up
As a child I had so many goals for my future
Hopeful for all of the amazing things I would do
I wonder what that child would say if she saw me now
Would she make different choices to ensure she would not end up like m
Would she be upset that her future is so dark?
Would she ever understand that I am trying to do my best?

Robbed of My Youth

I never did teenager things
The sneaking out of the house
The underage drinking
The hiding of a secret stash
The partying until we all pass out
The running away from a party gone wrong
The driving on a road trip to nowhere
The figuring out who I am

All of the experimenting was done by others
I just listened as they recounted their chronicles
Wishing that one day I too would have fun things to say
But I had overprotective parents that never let me out of their sight
And I was caught in the middle of two sides of an angry breakup
Other kids may start their own dating lives
Decide what they want in a potential significant other
I saw all of the things I never wanted to become
I saw all of the things I never wanted to see again

The constant fighting and name calling between them
The hatred, the resentment, the distrust
The talking to me about their personal love lives instead of getting a therapist
Watching the house I've lived in my entire life slowly disappear

Watching the image a supposed perfect family evaporate
away
Watching the adults around me acting like vicious
children
I had to grow up, I had to be there for my parents

I couldn't have my own boy problems
I couldn't obsess over little things like my hair or face or
eyes
I couldn't just invite my friends for a sleepover
I barely remember how I ever did any homework
Because my full time job was being the perfect daughter

And I wonder why I'm not fun at parties
Instead of standing on tables and dancing
I end up crying in a corner, feeling bad for feeling sad
Movies romanticize high school as this big coming-of-age
To learn about yourself and grow into someone better
The homecomings, the pep rallies, the proms
Supposedly major milestones in my young life
All of them meant nothing because I had more important
stuff
I couldn't worry about what dress I should wear to a
dance
I had to worry about lawyers and courts and paperwork
and all their reactions

I was people pleasing for so long that I do not know how
to please myself
And I thought something would change in college
But my parents' problems followed me there too

And I thought I can be independent after I was done with school
But I only knew how to avoid people and run away from my problems
And I thought I would just know what to do because everyone else seems to
But the secret is that no one ever stops growing and changing
There is still time for me to learn to be a fun person

Hardships of Friendships

Seeing friends was so easy back in college
I would run into you in the hallways after class
Or some college programming board event
And we'd talk and talk and talk
Go to the dining hall to eat
Hang out in someone's dorm
Just walk around the lake
And talk and talk and talk some more
Talk about hopes for the future
Where we will be once this all ends
Thinking that we will always be friends

But now I lie here waiting
Just staring at my screen
If you really do miss me
Why is it so hard to see me?
Oh you're busy that day
Well I can't make it a different day
You live so far away now
I don't even know what to do if you came here

So many decisions have to be made
We can go out to some nice restaurant
How fancy is too fancy?
Do you pay or do I?
Let's just split the bill
We can go to some mall
Walk around and shop

And everything will look great on you
And nothing will fit me perfectly
We can go to some show
But it's hard to reconnect in darkness
In the dark it's like you are not even there at all
We can talk about it when it ends

I'm vaccinated so don't really have to worry
I'm still the same me, I think I am
Are you the same you as before?
I haven't seen you since this whole mess began
And now we can meet
Just put in the work
Put in some thought
It's not so hard
When you're bored, hit me up
Anytime you're free message me
I'll be here on the other side of the phone

Maybe too much time has passed
Maybe I should have sent a "Happy New Year" text
Maybe you wouldn't like me anymore
Maybe it will never be the same as it was
Maybe I should have known this would happen
I haven't seen friends from high school since we graduated there
I haven't seen friends from youth group since our last meeting
I haven't seen friends from community theater since our final bow
I haven't seen friends from middle school since we all went to different high schools
Why would college friends be any different?
Maybe one of them would surprise me
And I'd finally have a best friend for life

The Struggle of Getting Out of Bed

Wasting away like a wilting wallflower
I sink deeper into my bed
It's softness comforts me
It's softness caresses me
It's softness consumes me
I am one with the covers

I cannot remember how long I've been laying here
I know I never want to leave
The outside world withers away
And with it
So too does the pain
The consequences
The people
The actions
The dreams
The love
The life

All of that evaporates away
All that remains
All that I hear
Are the cries of agony
The mournfulness of memories that are neither past nor present
They're the possible futures that I know I shall never see
Because I have the disease of being me
Those bright futures are wishes that will never come true

So they truly are passed

What could have been…
I should be…
If only I had…
Why bother trying?
What might have been…
I will never be…
If only I just…
Why bother risking?
What would have been…
I needed to be…
If only I was…
Why bother living?

These swirling sounds flood my brain
As I sink into the quicksand of of my own misery
Questioning whether I can finally reach quietness
They say there's still time to change
But I know it's all too late
Why prolong the inevitable
Why hope for a hopeless future
I cannot change the world
I cannot reverse time to make better choices

I lay as still as can be
Does that mean I will never be free
Of these thoughts that bind me
The anxiety that paralyzes me
The guilt that cripples me
The hopelessness that drains me

If the world is going to end anyway
Maybe it doesn't matter that I am not the perfect person I long to be
Maybe…
If this really is the end
I should at least see the sunrise
Feel the warmth of a new day
The possibility of something great
The possibility of something awful
No I'll just stay here
Too much can go wrong
If I leave the safety of my cocoon

I'm too scared to break out
I won't let myself become a butterfly
Why spread my wings only to be squashed
Or collected in a jar
Or spend eternity on someone else's wall
I'll stay in the in-between
I won't allow myself to change
I'll stay in my own vacuum of negativity forever
Except
I am getting hungry
Quick breakfast
Then I'll go back to sleep

Another Weekend Wasted

It cannot be Monday already
It absolutely cannot
How can 48 hours pass so quickly?
There were so many things to check off my to-do list
I didn't even open my planner yet
I can't even remember if I went outside yesterday
I struggle to remember the last time I ate anything

The entire time I had so many plans
I would finally clean up all of messes
I would finally figure out the whole closet situation
I would finally get up out of bed and see the sun shine

But in bed I stayed
It's just so comfy
With my weighted blanket pinning me down
And my head finding the perfect angle to rest on my
pillow
My phone becomes the only source of light I need
When I awake I wonder what I would do
And all that thinking is so tiring
That it puts me right back to sleep

With my eyes shut away from the world
My problems cease to exist
No, nothing can possibly be wrong
It feels so good to leave this material world behind

Have my soul float away to some better reality
I forget about the dishes that have to be cleaned
And the clothes that have to be folded
And all of the other chores that come with living on your own

In my dreams I can pretend I'm in my childhood home
That I never moved out and my parents never divorced
I can pretend I still talk to my friends from middle school and high school
And we still had the structure of a class schedule
I can pretend I became famous, an overnight success
Who is just so beautiful and talented and everyone knows my name

But my dreams have to pause for awhile
It is time to step back into the outside world
And I'm in no rush, I oversleep again
I slowly sit up on my bed as still as a statue
I don't wanna go
The world is scary and mean and takes everything away
I take a deep breath and I reluctantly rise
I remind myself my dreams will be here when I get back

Sad Eyes

Why am I sad?
I cannot give you an answer
I just feel like crying
Not that I want to
Not that I want my face to get all red
Not that I want my voice to become unintelligible
Not that I want you to look at me

Stop judging me
I guess you've never cried in public
Stop trying to make me feel better
I am too upset to be happy
Stop telling me stop
I don't know how

Everyone means well
Well I think they do
Do they actually want me to feel better?
Better that I'm sad
Sad that they might see themselves in my face
Facing the world and what it is
Is just too much to take in
In spite of the horrors of society
Society today is so unemotional and cold
Cold and dark are two things
Things that made me this way

My brain and its swirling thoughts
Never seem to tell my eyes
That there is no reason to cry
If they do, my eyes never listen
My eyes cannot hear the lies
No one knows if it will all be ok
No one knows if I will ever get better
No one knows if you will one day leave forever

I am supposed to be the epitome of greatness
I am supposed to be the one people look up to
I am supposed to be the light that radiates more light
All of these expectations
Jealous of a perfect version of myself
Someone that only exists in my head
Who makes me feel so horrible

I lay in the sanctuary of my bed
I stare at the chipped ceiling paint
My eyes wander to the broken pieces of tile
Clothes scatter the floor
Laundered and unlaundered become indistinguishable
A table that became a holding ground
Filled with lost items that have nowhere else to go
Drenched in absolute disorganization
One move and they all would fall
I let all of this happen
I let it all build up into a mountain
I let myself slowly waste away

I cry again
I cry for everything I am not
I cry for allowing myself to deteriorate
I cry for the life that I used to have
I cry for the life that never will be

I could change
But I would rather be in the predictability of despair
Than take a risk into unpredictability
Where I can actually get better, true
Or I can fail and become sadder than I already am
I cry again
Because I don't have the strength to turn on a light switch

Somewhere Where It's Sunny

I should live somewhere else
Where it doesn't get dark so early
Where it doesn't get so bitterly cold
Where it doesn't get so lonely

I should live where it is sunny
Somewhere out there
The outside world is full of pain
And all it is is just downpours of rain
But there has to be a place
Where everyone has a smiling face
They are not faking or pretending
They all genuinely have found their happy ending
It must exist
It must
It

I need this place to exist
To have some hope that it is out there
Where it scarcely rains
Only gentle rains
Only rains that make rainbows
Only rains for the aesthetic
Where it never storms
The clouds are white and fluffy
And they never turn gray
Ever

I don't care if the grass is greener
As long as it's not muddier
I don't think I'm asking for much here
It is so simple
At least it should be
I don't need a mansion
Or millions of useless things
I just want to be with people that like me
People that actually know my name
And when they like me
I will like me

I just need a change of scenery
Leave my problems back in the darkness
Make sure they don't follow me
Make sure that they stay locked without a key
Make sure they are forever away from me
It should be so easy

I need to get on with my life
And all of this trauma is really heavy
So I will throw it out
Bring some empty suitcase with me
Or just show up and see what happens
It should be better than here
Anything at all will be better than here
My life will be better away from here

Life Preserved By a Life Preserver

I didn’t want to look the lifeguard in the eye
I didn’t want to think about what I was about to do
I didn’t want to admit what I wished would happen

I didn’t think anyone would want to save me
I didn’t think anyone would care
I didn’t think anyone would come

I didn’t believe that I was worthy enough
I didn’t believe that I would change my mind
I didn't believe that I could feel good about something

I didn’t know what would happen
I didn’t throw the life preserver
I didn’t call out for help

But I did take the life preserver
But I did hold on as I was pulled to safety
But I did get onto that lifeboat

That should count for something

The Me My Eyes See

It started with a look
The look that looked back at me in the mirror
Where suddenly I did not recognize my own reflection
I know it's me
I am the only one standing here
A quick glance to make sure
And yes it is I
But something is different
Maybe my face got fatter
Or my hair got thinner
Or my nose got bigger
Or my teeth got yellower
No No No No
I'm still the same me
Not enough self esteem to call myself hot
But enough to call myself decent looking
Potentially cute if I put in some effort

It is my eyes that changed
They are still my eyes
Their color not quite brown
Not quite green
But it's just easier to say brown
With that annoying little freckle under my right eye
Yet I see my eyes look indescribably different
Eyebrows slightly more raised
With eyes piercing through the mirror
If I think hard enough maybe it will shatter

No that's not it
The eyes are not threatening
But very judgy
Judging what?
Judging who?

It's just this look
A look with unclear purpose
A look without motivation
A look that is looking for a reason
A look that is caught in disbelief
A look that I cannot look away from
I stand frozen at the prospect
That my eyes are looking
Searching
For something
For anything
An answer
A solution

It is I they are judging
And the world for making me this way
My eyes know that something is wrong
That I am not who I am supposed to be
I am not all I can be
There is so much more to me
Than the rest of me in the mirror

But my eyes are also kind
They have seen all that has happened
Things that I did
Things that were done to me

Things that I would rather forget
They know that it is not my fault
They know that I am just doing what I can
They know that I can be much more
They have hope for my future
They have hope for my well being
They have hope for my happiness

If only all the other parts of me can see what my eyes see
If my body and head can align with my eyes
They can move as one
Right now my eyes seem out of place
They know that things must change
But they are unfortunately confined to my face
They have no control over my legs
Or else I would be walking down another path
They have no control over my arms
Or else I would be creating great things
They have no control over my brain
Or else I would be thinking less about what if

I can only see my eyes in the mirror
I can only see the look when I look back
This feeling goes away as soon as I turn off the light
And the look is drowned out by the darkness
Even when I cannot see
My eyes are still looking
I just need to remind myself
To look in the mirror more
To see that I am so much more
Than what the rest of me believes

Going Up After Going Down

It is easy to tie a knot
It is easy to make it tight
It is easy to tangle up string
It is easy to make a mess

It is hard to untie a knot
It is hard to become loose
It is hard to straighten string without making more knots
It is hard to clean up the mess I've made

Falling is effortless
It can happen by accident
It can happen because I jump
It can happen from a big push

There is no thought involved with falling
Even if I had a thought
I'd be falling too fast to notice
It is just the action
It is just a constant downward motion
There is only way to stop
One way to end this suffering
Something needs to catch me
Someone needs to catch me
Until then I will keep going lower and lower

If I do stop falling
It will be quite a long journey up
Of course the elevator will be broken
No easy way up
I have to take the stairs
Going upstairs is harder than going downstairs
I might just go down because that is what I'm used to
I should take a step up
But it hurts too much to try

I'm afraid of what I'll find as I reach the top of the steps
I might fall down again
I need to stop thinking like that
Yes I will fall again
No need to worry about that
I must remember that there is life beyond the fall
I don't have to live in darkness
There are a lot of steps to climb
I honestly can't say if I'll make it
But I do know that each step will get me closer to the light

Scar Tissue Pain

There is a pain inside of me
But if you asked
I could not tell you where
There are no physical damages
No bruises or bumps or lumps
No cuts or scrapes or blood
Just invisible scars
Hidden away from the outside world

I want to scream
I want to scream so loud
I want to scream so loud to force it to come out
I want to shout
I want to shout so much
I want to shout so much that it hurts me not to

I want it to leave me
I want to not feel anymore
I want to go back to before

But it never leaves me
But I will feel it forever more
But I cannot go back to before

Before I was sick
Before I felt so awful
Before I knew that anything was wrong

And while I am cured
Those scars prove it
The nerves are still regenerating
They know something happened
When they grow, they send me reminders
I wish those reminders would be less painful

It is hard to move on with these scars
I can never truly get over it
Because it still hurts
And I get stuck in the past
Transported to a time I'd rather forget

And then I take a deep breath
I am not where I used to be
I am not who I used to be
I no longer have that sickness within me
I stand tall and undefeated

I send reminders to myself
My hair has grown back
So much time has passed
I am completely unrecognizable
In the best possible ways

The pain will never go away
Some days it might be less
Some days it might be more
Some days I may forget that it ever happened
Some days I may constantly go through the memories
Some days I feel like I am in a comedy
Some days I feel like I am in a tragedy

And while it may be hard to understand
The outside world may never understand
Sometimes I can barely understand
Why this all happened to me
How I can bare to even keep going
Where to place the blame
What I ever did to deserve this
Who I would have been if it never happened
When it all started to go wrong
When it all started to go right

The scars will always be there
The pain will always be there
The past will always be there
But I can still look to the future

I feel
I remember
I scream
I shout
I breathe
I open my eyes
And I get on with my day
The pain is still in me
But it is only one part of a different me

State of Mattering

The rain will drop
It will eventually stop
While it won't disappear
The rain will come and go like my tears

The feeling never goes away
Not completely
It just evaporates
It goes into a different state of mattering
The things that bring you down
Will cease to mean anything at all
It simply evaporates

It can be comforting to have your own personal rain cloud
At least it's yours
No one can take it away
However much it hurts
It hurts more thinking what you would do without it
The struggle to shelter yourself
Once you find it
That perfect awning
The umbrella that doesn't fold up when it gets too windy
A rainbow colored umbrella hat even
But then what do you do
Stay under that cover
Or run back into the storm
Because at least in the storm you are away from the world

I logically know the rain will evaporate
I just have to see it
I may have too many tears
It's blinding to the sunlight
Don't be afraid of what comes after the night
The unknown is scary and at least the rain is known
It's something I own
Without it I don't know who I am
Just a person alone
Covered in drops of tears

I throw umbrellas and raincoats away
Cover me in rain drops
Here is where I'll forever stay
Even if the rain evaporates
I can't tell
I won't be able to tell
I'll still think it's raining
Even if it isn't
I'll summon it
I'll call upon it
Come back
Rain down on me again
It's the only comfort I have in my lonely life

It only evaporates
Just goes into a different state of matter
If it doesn't completely disappear why bother
It'll be here always
So I might as well always be in it too
In the midst of the mist of rain

Then someone comes along
Seeing me drenched in tear drops
That refuse to dry off my face
Then they turn to me and say
The rain will come back again
But you have to remember my friend
It will evaporate once more
This time a little easier than before

The rain drops don't have to stay in your eyes
Tell the rain your goodbyes
All you see in front of you are just internal lies
And I know you try
Just please believe me when I say
That soon you'll realize, hey
It really is a bright colorful beautiful sunny day

The First Night I Looked At You

The universe is random
Things happen and happen and happen
I can try to find a reason
Try to put together signs
Decipher some code
Find some purpose as for why
Why the good
Why the bad
Why the nothing
Why the everything
But I guess it doesn't matter
Because now I have you

There are so many what ifs
What if you didn't have a long day at work?
What if you decided not to go to that cafe to clear your head?
What if you stayed back west and never moved here?
What if I didn't get out of bed?
What if I decided to go to a different cafe?
What if I stayed at home and kept feeling sorry for myself?
I'll never know if it was fate or destiny or chance
That are eyes happened to meet
How we looked at each other
A look that lasted a lifetime

And somehow I said hi
And for reasons I will never understand
You said hi too

And the rest of the world ceased to exist
Even though it was dark outside
You were so full of light
I don't even remember the rest of the words
But somehow you liked me enough
Or you wanted me enough
Or you found me hot enough
Or cute enough
Or maybe my personality was good enough
That we promised to meet again

I wasn't expecting you
I wasn't looking for you
And yet you appeared before my eyes
Is this what happens when one goes outside?
The world gives you a gift
To show that you are on the right path
And yes bad things happen
But if it wasn't for those things
I wouldn't be where you were that night
Maybe I would have met someone equally as good
But it would not have been you
Everything had to happen the way it did
So we can be in the same movement
Oh how forever grateful I will be
For whatever force of nature brought us together

Diiiinnngg

The sound of instant happiness
The sound of someone out there
Out in this cold dark universe
Out comes a glimmer of light
Someone cares about me
Someone took precious time
Away from viral videos
Away from soul sucking work
Away from their daily lives
To text ME!

The sound of an equally lost person reaching out back to me
The sound of someone curious
The sound of someone bored
The sound of someone concerned
The sound of someone bewitched
The sound of someone longing for connection
The sound meaning that I am not alone

The sound I can never get tired of
The sound that shows you care
The sound I will be forever grateful for
The sound that stops the world
The sound that makes the world brighter

I worry it will be the last sound I hear from you
If you figure out you would rather ding someone else
That I am not happy enough to be around
That I do not reciprocate your love enough
That someone else has a prettier picture

That I am not worthy enough
That I said something wrong
That I responded too quickly
That I responded too slowly

What if you hate me?
What if it is such a drag to be around me?
What if I am not pleasant enough?
What if I am too much for you?
What if I am too emotional?
What if you resent me?
What if you never want to see me again?

Maybe I should just not read it
Maybe it is better not to know
Maybe I can just pretend it is something nice
Maybe I should just throw my phone away
Maybe it is better to leave it alone
Maybe I can just pretend I never heard it

DIIIINNNGG

I take a deep breath
It's you again
I read the message:
Heart-Eyed Emojis

Everything in the universe is good
Filled with joy of a reminder that I am loved
My smile takes up my entire face
I am at peaceful serenity once again

When I See You and Feel You Again

I awake with a smile
It's you
You're still here
With me
Just me
Only me
With only you
Just us
Together

Your arms are so warm
I hold onto you tightly
Afraid you will disappear if I let go
If I stop squeezing
You might evaporate into nothingness
If I stop touching
You might turn into a figment of my imagination
If I stop cuddling
You might cease to exist

Your arms reassure me
Your arms validate me
Your arms comfort me
Your arms keep me safe
Your arms let me know it's ok
Your arms transport me from my reality

To somewhere where we can just be

But I have to let go
But you have to go
And I am at peace
You are not here to save me
You are not here to rescue me
My problems are still within me
So are my thoughts and my past
Nothing went magically away
You may not be Prince Charming
And I am definitely no Princess either
Yet in your arms and looking in your eyes
Despite of everything I am and everything I am not
I get something better than a basic fairytale life
I see something real

Where is the Confetti?

There is a mystery I have to solve
Something gnawing away at me
If I don’t find the answer
My very existence will be meaningless

Where is the confetti?
Where is the big brass band?
Where is the party in my honor?
Where are the banners and the signs?
Where is the big parade to celebrate?
Where is the light that is supposed to shine?
Where is the rainbow across the sky?
Where is someone to shout from the rooftops?
Where is the celebration now that I am better?
I don’t see it
I can’t find it

How do I know then?
Am I happy yet?
Have I reached the end of my worries?
Is there more I have to do?
When can I see the end of the quest?
Can I finally relax?

There is no switch that goes off
There is no obvious finish line
There is no map to tell me where I am
There is no end to this endless maze

I'm trying here
But maybe it's too much
Or too little

I want to be done already
I want to be happy
I want to have my happy ending
I think I do
Why would I want to keep being sad?
You think I like crying?
These tears are not tears of joy
They are not for your attention
Maybe I will always be sad

I just want some kind of confirmation
Send an email or carrier pigeon
Something to let me know
Something that says one hundred percent positive
Some kind of divine intervention
Anything
That I am finally going to be ok from now on
That I suffered enough and that it will only be good now
That I can finally stop crying for the rest of my life
That I can walk into the sunset and never have to look back

Everyone else I see
The old couples holding hands
Children running around
Dog walkers
Runners
Cashiers
Everyone just seems so happy

They must all know some secret
Does my sadness make them uncomfortable?
Are they laughing at me?
Is that why they're all smiling?
Maybe the maximum amount of happy people is reached
And I'm just left out of it all

Reminder to Look

Friendly reminder
When the days get darker
Now I'm not trying to sound cliche
But there really is no other way
To say all I can say

Just waking up makes you a winner
Maybe you're a little less thinner
Maybe you get another wrinkle
Maybe your eye has a little less twinkle

When you wake up
That means you are alive
That means you have another chance
That means you can do something

We don't know if the sun will come out tomorrow
Do not let yourself get drowned by all the what-ifs
Think about the now

Look out the window
There is no rush
But when you get out of bed
Preferably when there is still daylight
Whether it is sunny or cloudy
Windy or stormy
Even if the apocalypse is upon us
Look

Really look out at the window
Take it all in
No matter what you see
The good or the bad
Or the in between
You were here to see it
And there will be nothing like it again

www.ingramcontent.com/pod-product-compliance
Lightning Source LLC
Chambersburg PA
CBHW051738130826
49812CB00033B/915
* 9 7 8 9 3 5 7 4 4 0 7 8 3 *